Götterdämmerung

ESSENTIAL POETS SERIES 280

Guernica Editions Inc. acknowledges the support
of the Canada Council for the Arts and the Ontario Arts Council.
The Ontario Arts Council is an agency of the Government of Ontario.
We acknowledge the financial support of the Government of Canada.

Götterdämmerung

Len Gasparini

GUERNICA
EDITIONS

TORONTO • CHICAGO • BUFFALO • LANCASTER (U.K.)
2020

Michael Mirolla, editor
Cover and Interior Design: Rafael Chimicatti
Guernica Editions Inc.
287 Templemead Drive, Hamilton (ON), Canada L8W 2W4
2250 Military Road, Tonawanda, N.Y. 14150-6000 U.S.A.
www.guernicaeditions.com

Distributors:
Independent Publishers Group (IPG)
600 North Pulaski Road, Chicago IL 60624
University of Toronto Press Distribution (UTP),
5201 Dufferin Street, Toronto (ON), Canada M3H 5T8
Gazelle Book Services, White Cross Mills
High Town, Lancaster LA1 4XS U.K.

First edition.
Printed in Canada.

Legal Deposit – Third Quarter
Library of Congress Catalog Card Number: 2019949236
Library and Archives Canada Cataloguing in Publication
Title: Götterdämmerung / Len Gasparini.
Other titles: Works. Selections
Names: Gasparini, Len, author.
Series: Essential poets ; 280.
Description: Series statement: Essential poets series ; 280
Poems and essays.
Identifiers: Canadiana 20190176121
ISBN 9781771835473 (softcover)
Classification: LCC PS8563.A7 A6 2020 I DDC C811/.54—dc23

I sang ...

> and the song, stained with the stain of chlorophyll
> was sharp as a whistle of grass
> in my green blood.
>
> —*P.K. Page*

*To the memory of my father;
and to Lisa—for her patience
and encouragement*

Contents

I

II Three Essays

I

Götterdämmerung

I

In 2018, I saw by the false dawn's light
the first robin of spring.
It lay on my doorstep. Dead.
If signs are taken for wonders,
what sign was this?

The signs environ us.
As a tellurian of the Anthropocene,
can you not tell the signs
by sight, smell, hearing, taste, and touch?
We have despoiled Nature with pollution
beyond the point of no solution.
We have created a second Nature
in the image of the first
so as not to believe that we live in paradise.
(From Mother Earth to Earth Mother
to Mother Nature only women know *nurture*.)
Nature is full of surprises.

The signs environ us.
Earth, air, water, and fire.
We live, and we expire.
Acid rain, acid rain, go away,
don't come again another day.
We'll go to the woods no more,
the trees have been clear-cut.

I see condo-mania under construction
in a deep excavation a city block square ...
Sky-high decadence, says an advertisement.
("buildung supra buildung supra buildung")
Termite towers
Montreal Toronto Vancouver
I hear a pneumatic drill. I smell an oil spill.
I remember the taste of road tar I chewed as a kid.
By a streambank I touch the seedpod of a touch-me-not.

The natural world resides in the rhythms,
variations, and combinations of certain patterns:
the spirals of pine cones, fish scales, seashells;
the zigzags of lightning, the geometry of spiderwebs;
the symmetry of snowflakes, the wavy lines of surf;
frostwork, palm trees grazing the horizons ...

Is technology conditioning us
to become an abstraction
in a virtual environment?
Are you a mere mechanism
in a mechanistic universe?
Have we all lost touch with life?
We are in danger of dehumanizing ourselves.
Nobody dances anymore.
Nobody dances anymore.
We have nothing in hand but our cell phones.

For global warming read GLOBAL WARNING.
We drove past the first sign years ago
when gasoline and diesel fuel were cheaper.
Climate change: a euphemism
that sounds like a video game.

Greenhouse effect: a misnomer.
Ditto greenhouse gas; moreover,
the etymon of *chaos* is *gas*.
Do we need to make new cars every year?
Earth Day 1970. "We have met the enemy and he is us."

"The poetry of earth is never dead," said Keats.
"The whole earth is our hospital," said T.S. Eliot.
"The earth is an Indian thing," said Jack.
"Nobody owns the earth," said Bill.

The earth is licking its festering sores.
The earth is suffering from overpopulationpollution.
"We are a plague on the earth," said Sir David
Attenborough.

Garden gnomes are picking the tomatoes.
Farming has gone to pot.
Ill from breathing herbicides, the scarecrow
now lies in a woodlot.
Swamps and marshes are drained for farming ...
the water table has dropt, harming
plants and wildlife—and it is too goddamn late,
too goddamn late to replant this earth.

In a run-down city run by hucksters
there is the Ojibway Nature Centre.
Alongside it runs Matchette Road—
(the locals call it "hatchet road")
notorious for its roadkill:
raccoons, turtles, snakes, skunks, squirrels ...

While we were watching the incoming tide,
a stale, smelly air blew onto the shore
from an ocean polluted with plastic.
Farther along the shore
lay the scarred carcass of a manatee.

The waters of the world are bleeding
blue-green algal blooms breeding
dead zones, dead zones, dead zones ...

If the spark of life was a blue-green accident,
consider the binary fission of bacteria
chemically beneficial and bad, omnipresent
as the sun, the moon, photosynthesis ...

Let us poison bioprospectors vaunting
biopiracy's flagship flaunting
skulls and crossbones, skulls and crossbones ...

Psychedelia started with the Twist.
We had a saying; it went like this:
There's a humungous fungus among us.
There's a humungous fungus among us.

Wake up, baby boomers, Generation Xers!
Have you heard the news?
We are rocking the balance of nature.
At the twilight's last gleaming,
your grandchildren will be gasping for oxygen
like herring caught in a gill net.

We who are so very human
are very animal. We must not deny
the other animals. Their history
is our history. If we kick them
to the bottom of the abyss,
to the bottom
of the abyss
we ourselves go.

In the recurrence of time,
life seeks to preserve itself,
but life seeks also to perish.
Do you perceive this chthonic force?
I think the world is one big stomach
fed by tooth and claw
compared with factory farming
and mechanized slaughterhouses.
Five out of four Americans are obese.

Being latest in the ascent of life,
from the jellyfish to the mastodon,
it follows that we must be
the least perfect form of life.
(Not *Homo sapiens* but *Homo* sap.)
Humans don't exist anymore—only their symptoms.

So far, we've succeeded in polluting
the planet, dooming ourselves
and our creaturely cousins to extinction.
Nothing succeeds like success.
Which planet is next?

II

To stand in my father's garden
fragrant after a spring rain
and feel the wet earth under my bare feet
is a soul massage so sensuously deep
that I know how a flower must feel
when it puts forth a blossom.

My father spied a garter snake;
a frog protruded from its mouth.
His first reaction was instinctive,
and he wriggled the frog out.
He could not but wonder afterwards
if he had interfered with nature.

My closest communion with nature came
when I spent the summer studying
the life cycle of the praying mantis
on the cedar shrubs in my backyard.

A child once asked me: "How is it that flowers, which are so pretty, don't sing like birds?"
"They do sing," I replied, "but we don't know how to hear them."

Earth has few secrets from the birds.
From the poles to the tropics,
birds hold us in their spell;
mesmerize us with their music.
If you ever see the skeleton of a bird,
you will know how completely it is still flying.

Once upon a Maytime twilight,
in the deepening gloom of a wooded ravine,
I heard the eerie song of the veery
(a songbird seldom seen)
whose liquid, reedy, downward spiraling song
resonated as if the bird
carried its own echo within itself.

Approaching the grasslands
near Val Marie, Saskatchewan
for the first time, on foot,
as the day dawned with a cloudless sky,
I saw how time is subordinate
to space, and suddenly I longed to be
that western meadowlark—
a blaze of pure being
perched on a barbed-wire fence,
singing its melodious song.

We were ambling along the marsh boardwalk.
The sunrise was like a ripe peach.
"O look!" she pointed. "Look over there!"
A great blue heron rose from behind some cattails,
and, with his head and neck folded back,
flew over Point Pelee as if
he were taking the sky with him.

Under the curve of a cliff swallow's flight
glides the very curvature of the earth.

Greenpeace International. June 23rd
        MORE THAN ONE-THIRD
OF NORTH AMERICA'S NATIVE BIRD SPECIES
ARE AT IMMEDIATE RISK OF EXTINCTION

III

In North America
beauty is born of the rain.
We live in the shade
of the world's biggest, tallest, and oldest trees.

In the northwest Pacific rainforest, rain is regnant,
rain sets the theme, dripping
from leaves, cones, and branches, trickling
down tree trunks, flowing among ferns,
mosses, mushrooms, lichens ... soaking
into the forest floor.
There is rain
on the cloud-topped Douglas firs,
rain on the Sitka spruces
with their drooping branches,
rain on the hemlocks
encrusted with lichens,
rain on our faces,
rain on our hands which are bare.
There is rain
on a gloomy green solitude.
The sound of the ocean is unheard,
but a rivulet gives rhythm to the rain.
We are sinking into the atmosphere
of the rainforest. Our sylvan faces
are wet with the rain.
We appear to each other out of bark.
Everything in us is scented
with rain, rain, rain.
Green is the rain; green is the beauty
born of the rain.

This is the forest primeval,
and still it is to MacMillan Bloedel—
a tree parasite capable
of dooming British Columbia to a treeless hell. *(1993)*

In nature, nothing is wasted.
Stumbling over
an old mossed log in the forest,
my son discovers its underside
half buried in humus
teeming with fungi, seedlings, insects ...
and is amazed by the life
its decay has created.

The beauty and fragrance of a Christmas tree
decorated with ornaments and lights
(originally the embodiment
of a vegetation ceremony),
is the closest some people come to Nature.

The leaves of trees
use quantum mechanics for photosynthesis,
my grandson who majors in physics told me.
I said: Nature is its own metaphor.

Along the Mississippi flyway
the autumn woods are stained
with the colors of migrating birds
that once sang in them and nested.

I planted a linden sapling.
It will surely outlive me,
though I hope to see

its fragrant yellow flowers
attract the first honeybee.

Medieval alchemists
saw the union of opposites
under the symbol of the linden tree.
    Unter der linden, an der heide,
    da unser zweier bette was,
    da muget ir vinden schöen beide
    gebrochen bluomen unde gras.

The wind is a tree's only chance
to make music and dance.

Greenpeace International. October 24th
    TWO AND A HALF MILLION TREES
ARE CUT DOWN DAILY THROUGHOUT THE WORLD

What is a weed?
A weed is a wildflower that blossoms
to better the earth with beauty.
A wildflower is any flowering plant
that grows out of place because it claims
ever more living space for its species.
Weeds are people's idea, not nature's.
Long live the weeds and the wilderness too.
Dandelions are sunning my lawn.

Pistil and stigma, stamen and anther ...
We depend on flowering plants.
To life's enigma they grow earth's answer.
Certain plants are sensitive indicators
that air pollution poisons pollinators,

without which the future has no destination.
A flower will do anything to get pollinated.

Weeds seem to multiply overnight.
Heaven knows we hoe them often enough,
uprooting or poisoning
the common and the troublesome ones.
Still they survive the hoe, the herbicide,
holding their ground as though they own it,
disfiguring our lawns, choking our flowers,
thriving even in crevices of concrete.
It is not their appearance that offends us,
but lack of cultivation;
the way they invade our gardens
with such vigorousness.
Yet who are we to deny them wild growth?
Come, let us spare their weedy lives,
let us call them by their proper names:
lady's thumb, toadflax, shepherd's purse, goldenrod ...

According to the Doctrine of Signatures
in the seventeenth century,
plants proclaimed their medicinal properties
by some aspect of their appearance.
The birthwort's flower resembles a uterus.
It was reputed to facilitate childbirth;
but its stems contain a dangerous toxin.
In the clefts of rocks the saxifrage grows.
Its roots were used for treating kidney stones.

Certain herbs could ward off evil:
Trefoil, vervain, St. Johnswort, and dill
Hinder witches of their will.

Let's not forget nepenthe, mandrake, moly
which the ancients deemed magical and holy;
or the shrub *Erythroxylon coca*:
the source of pure cocaine—an alkaloid
that fills the void and fortifies the brain.
Opium poppy, magic mushroom, peyote cactus
make the senses confuse their functions.
I could smell the color purple …
I could see the music, hear the dance …
    tra-la-la

Erratic November weather conditions prevail
as temperatures fluctuate daily in Detroit
and in Windsor, Ontario (city of parking lots)
where a milkweed's swollen seedpods
have yet to burst open
because of ground-level ozone pollution.
To the survival of the monarch butterfly
this is crucial.

IV

As time and space become compressed,
we seldom socialize in the flesh.
There will be selective breeding,
robot sex dolls for the unchosen;
and for dignitaries: deep freezing
instead of crowded cemeteries.

The Judeo-Christian Bible, the Koran …
O the vain anthropocentrism
and theanthropism of man.

Do we need myths? Should these bones live?
The computer runs algorithms
but the psyche's still primitive.

Love's ever spiraling ouroboros
moves the cosmos. The life of the cosmos
resides in rhythm. The cosmos dances.
Playing a one-nighter at Mudbugs Saloon,
Jerry Lee Lewis said: "If you don't dance,
you don't know what happens."

In the afterbirth of the third millennium
does it strike you as medieval
that we still have a pope,
kings and queens, princes, princesses
who live in great comfort and luxury
while the rest of us pay taxes.
If ecology were a religion,
blessèd it would be to conserve
the habitat of the monarch butterfly
from greenbelt development.
Nature has done so much for the earth and we so little.

In an age of rockets refueling on stars,
when humans are planning to visit Mars
and paving the jungles for guided tours,
my travel urge met with an inner resistance.

All of us have one trait: we are centripetal—
presumably a way of protecting the core.
We hold our hand in front of the candle,
and live in a veiled light, in the specious present,
taking no account of the past or the future.

Logos bogus, hocus-pocus,
perception itself is disputable.

(In a Louisiana bayou
glimmering with phosphorescence,
I perceived the hypercathected reality
of the physical world.)

Reality is said to begin
outside verbal language.
I suspect that mathematicians know this.
The theorems of mathematics prove it.
Digit. Digital. Digital divide. Can you dig it?

*The reality that once existed in relation to us
has lost its significance and has thus assumed
an uncanny reality unto itself ...*

It is the imaged word, creation's word,
the word as metaphor,
the word as art that produces form
that derives from color ...
Yes, Rembrandt, the natural world is ordered by color,
iridescence, mimicry too.
A rose is not a rose unless you know
how many petals it has.

Let us look at Michelangelo's fresco:
The Creation of Adam—an anthropocentric myth
of its time, in which the forefingers
of two reclining figures almost touch ...
(At the zoo one day, I proffered a grape
to an anthropoid ape.

I was amazed at how gently she took it
with her thumb and forefinger).

   Charles Darwin's wife (who bore ten children) asked him
if apes mated in a missionary position.
   They don't mate in captivity, he said.

From the tip of a melting iceberg
to the ice sculpture of a polar bear
(life-size almost, and glittering)
on display in a city park.
The laying on of human hands ablates it.

As the twig is bent, so grows the tree,
as the saying goes—or, genetically,
to codify, modify, manipulate
the double helix, and dice with fate—
or, gladly, to embrace *Amor fati*;
or to accept the concept of *esho funi*;
or to regard the world as an illusion
from which we must free ourselves
in order to find salvation;
or to praise *Drosophila*, a fruit fly.

In this wireless world, life is a matter
of hours—full ones and empty ones,
this is the whole of psychology
in a pharmaceutical drug-saturated society.
In this digital age which advances
progressively backwards
in a pageantry of gadgetry,
we no longer know what to think.
What makes us try to give expression to anything?

(I know you believe you understand
what you think I said, but I am not sure
you realize that what you heard
is not what I meant.)
We do not believe. We fear.

Warriors will war with warriors
via cyber weaponry.
Clausewitz's dictum hovers over
the twenty-first century:
"War is a human endeavour."
Or will everlasting peace come to the earth
when we humans no longer inhabit it?
(What is history? Read further:
the justification of mass murder.)

As the global commons become commodified,
workers will work like worker bees and ants.
Breeders will breed, as if by blind will,
incapable of cognition ...

In the present time of present things,
what is your relation to nature?
If nature becomes godlike, will it not also
be demonic and destroy us
with the same mindless brutality
with which we destroy wildlife?
If the brute is necessary,
who is to be the brute?
There must be aspects of our nature
that neither Faust nor Mephisto could foresee.

Because we are subject to the second
thermodynamic law of existence,
we blunder into entropy
by trying to anticipate or control nature,
like "the blind men and the elephant."

The windy dawn is cold and damp.
The land is unfit for food crops.
The air is too smoggy to breathe.
The water is unsafe to drink.
The river nymphs have vanished.
The sky is red and lowering. Let fire purify
the whole anthropogenic mess.

(Scatter my ashes on the lone prairie
where the coyotes howl and the wind blows free.)

That which lives is something other than that which thinks.
"D'où venons nous? Que sommes nous? Où allons nous?"
We have stepped out of Nature
and into the heart of darkness
which is Absolute Reality.

March 2018—December 2019

Notes on Götterdämmerung

The title of the poem is taken from Richard Wagner's fourth and final opera of *Der Ring des Nibelungen*. "Götterdämmerung" translates as "twilight of the gods." The poem has nothing to do with gods and mythology but everything to do with the Anthropocene and the "twilight" of the natural world.

I.

Cf. Eliot, *Gerontion*.
V. Milosz, *Three Talks on Civilization*.
Cf. Housman, *We'll to the Woods No More*.
V. Kerouac, *The Subterraneans*.
Cf. Joyce, *Finnegans Wake*.
Cf. Dostoevsky, *Notes from Underground*, II, x.
The quote from the American cartoonist Walt Kelly, creator of the comic strip *Pogo,* appeared on a poster for the first Earth Day, April 22, 1970.
The Ojibway Nature Centre is located in Windsor, Ontario.
V. Key, *The Star-Spangled Banner*.
Cf. Benn, *Prose, Essays, Poems*.

II.

V. Strindberg, *Graveyard Reveries*.
Point Pelee is located in SE Ontario where it juts into Lake Erie. It forms the southernmost tip of mainland Canada. In 1918, Point Pelee became the first national park in Canada to be established for conservation.
The four lines in Middle High German are from a love poem by Walther von der Vogelweide (c.1170-c.1230).

III.

Cf. Attenborough, *The Private Life of Plants*.
Cf. Hopkins, *Inversnaid*.
V. Sir Walter Scott, *The Nativity Chant*.
Cf. Huxley, *Plant and Planet*.

IV.

Jerry Lee Lewis, U.S. rock-and-roll singer and pianist.
The phrases *Amor fati* and *esho funi* mean, respectively, "love of one's fate," and "the Oneness of Life and its Environment."
This is *Drosophila melanogaster*, a small two-winged fruit fly used extensively in genetic research because of its large chromosomes and rapid rate of reproduction.
Karl von Clausewitz, Prussian general and military theorist. He wrote *On War*, which had a marked influence on strategic studies in the 19th and 20th centuries.
Cf. Anderson, *The Horn Island Logs of Walter Inglis Anderson*.
V. John Godfrey Saxe, the title of a Hindu fable.
The line in French in the poem's final stanza is the title of a painting by Paul Gauguin.

A Visit to Edgar Allan Poe's Cottage in the Bronx

Under an ashen-grey October sky
the drone of daytime traffic followed me
as I walked from the Kingsbridge Road subway station
to Edgar Allan Poe's cottage
in the Bronx.

The white, one-and-a-half story cottage
had a veranda, windows with green shutters;
frame-built, unlike the house of Usher.
Inside, the rooms were small, the ceiling low.
I wondered how tall was Poe.

There were souvenirs aplenty.
A bronze bust of Poe surveyed one room,
a stuffed raven surveyed another.
Have Your Very Own Black Cat: $4.00 each.
Did I expect a free frisson?

Poe himself would have shuddered.
What demon had tempted me here?
I climbed a dimly lighted staircase
whose narrowness was claustrophobic,
and stumbled on his tubercular wife's deathbed.

Then felt I like some intruder. The reality
seemed so unreal. Did I imagine the air tainted?
I had journeyed here alone
to pay homage to Poe
in that month of all months in the year.

Homage to Albert Franck

Who remembers Toronto's Cabbagetown in the 1960s?
only Hugh Garner, Juan Butler, Ted Plantos,
that I know of, and me. The rest of you
probably never heard of Albert Franck—
an artist who painted winter scenes
of Cabbagetown in deep colors
with black-and-white streaks and shadings,
and gave street names to his paintings.
Ah, those old run-down red-brick Victorian-style houses,
snow-covered streets, backyards, and alleys
were once a neighborhood—a consecration of white
in wintertime, an illumination of things hidden.

The Flying Sleigh

There's a flowering of colors in Chagall's work,
color within color. He paints the paint.
                    —E.M. Bruski

In Marc Chagall's *The Flying Sleigh*,
a huge red-combed white rooster harnessed to a yellow
                                                    sleigh
is conveying the sleigh driver clad in green,
and a woman all in red (with one breast exposed) holding
                                                    a child
above the snow-covered rooftops of a Russian village
into the night sky where a blue flute player dances ...

An enchanting dreamscape of happiness
except for two frightened faces peering
through a small cleft in the sky.
(Why do these faces look afraid?)

When I study *The Flying Sleigh*
I feel a rush of nostalgia for my childhood.
Graven on my memory is the image I have of mine.

A snowy December night.
My mother and I are walking to my grandparents' house.
Halfway there she stops to chat in Italian
with an old gypsy woman named Gioconda.

The three of us stand under a lamppost
on the southeast corner
of Elliott and Marentette streets.
Through the lamppost's aureate glow
I gaze up at the night sky—a crystal chandelier
of snowflakes falling, falling …
I'm enraptured by the beauty and mystery of it.

Childhood builds its own shrines,
and these remain untarnished and infrangible
to the end of one's time.

The Reality of Things

Many years ago, in Detroit,
I attended a poetry reading by Karl Shapiro.
Between poems he mentioned the logic of metaphor:
"If you're hunting for Indian arrowheads,
look for a stone that wanted to fly."

(The imaginative comprehension
of this figure of speech must be immediate,
intuitive—otherwise you miss
the meaning. Metaphor is a mode
of consciousness. It can't be taught.)

I was never quite the same after that,
so I took to smoking marijuana.
It is said that King Solomon
wrote the *Song of Songs*. He had 700 wives
and 300 concubines—and so little time.

From Shapiro, I learned that poetry
gains strength by dashing itself against
the reality of things, like his "Manhole Covers."
So I became an initiate when I found
a cicada shell that had sung itself utterly away.

Once Upon an Autumn

My father once read a poem to me:
"Come, Little Leaves," by George Cooper.
I had to memorize it, and stand up to recite it
in front of my grade school class—
a daunting task for a ten-year-old.

I read the poem aloud over and over.
It elegized autumn
in a hauntingly innocent way;
and consisted of five quatrains in closed couplets,
which aided me in learning it.

More than half a century later
I still know the poem by heart.
On an autumn day
I remember more of childhood
than at any other time of year.

Audition Colorée

Arthur Rimbaud
may have colored
the vowels,
but a parrot talks
in tropical
colors.

1954

Chasing used auto parts—
going along for the ride
with my Uncle Leo
to auto-wrecking yards
in Detroit, Port Huron, Toledo.

I was a kid who read comic books,
billboards, Burma-Shave signs,
and rode a Schwinn bicycle;
spent most of my summer vacation
collecting old license plates

I unscrewed from wrecked cars
from faraway places: Utah,
Prince Edward Island, Idaho,
Wyoming, New Mexico, Tennessee …
That's how I learned geography.

Nowadays, automobiles
all look the same. Alas!
Discovering a beautiful old car
in a wrecking yard
is a thing of the past.

Coda

After the poetry reading,
the polite applause; the lectern, the microphone,
the glass of water abandoned,
she walked up behind me and touched my arm ...

We were born and raised in the same city—
twenty-eight years apart.
Slowly, strange coincidences aside,
our roots began to intertwine.

Drum Majorette

Strutting in a sequined fringe skirt
and white knee-high boots,
her legs command a marching band.

With speed, control, and poise
she twirls, whirls her baton counterclockwise,
hurls it high into the air,

then catches it on the fly—
everybody gazing at
the winged harmony of her hands.

Simon Says

Let us take the word *simony*
and make it a simile,
like Xtians on Xanax
wearing Halloween halos.

The Birth of a Banana Leaf

Have you ever observed
the slow, slightly moist unfurling
of a banana leaf?

Day after summer day for a whole week
in subtropical sunlight
the new leaf unrolls its fragile scroll
until the green ink of chlorophyll
suffuses it completely.

It arches itself among
older, larger, wind-torn leaves
on the scar-braided trunk.

Now press your face to the leaf's smooth surface,
smell and touch its birth—delivered
by photosynthesis.

My Favorite Flower

With a magnifying glass I study
the parts of my favorite flower:
a purple bearded iris.
I have a honeybee's-eye view.

I focus on one of its falls—
a downward drooping sepal that feels
like a smooth, soft fold of skin
veined with nectar-guides and yellow bristles.

Behind three sepals stand three erect petals
or standards. The calyx and corolla
form the perianth. I am an explorer
amid two whorls of floral parts

in a world of color and scent.
I smell the flower's purple fragrance.
Like a bumblebee probing for nectar,
I probe the pollen-laden anther,

the pistil's sticky stigmatic lip.
So many parts to botanize: stamen,
style arm, spathe, carpel, ovary ...
O where is the nectary hidden?

My fingertips are dusted with pollen.
Do I dare to quench my thirst
without pollinating an iris in return?
My favorite flower flavors Bombay Sapphire gin.

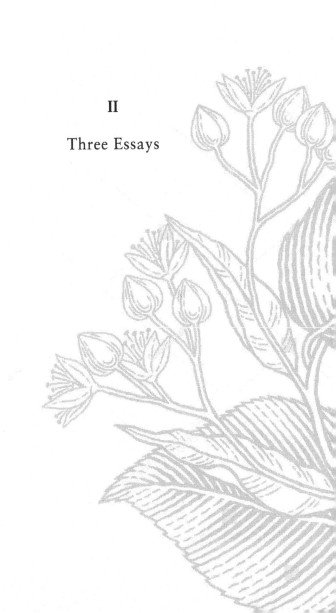

II

Three Essays

A Refuge from Rage: Milton Acorn and His Poetry

1.

I first met Milton Acorn at a poetry reading he gave in Windsor, Ontario in March 1973. I remember the date because it was his fiftieth birthday. He had been invited to read by a cadre of young activists who ran a small bookshop (with posters of Malcolm X and Che Guevara in the window) that specialized in national liberation literature. The shelves were stocked with such items as the *Peking Review*, Herbert Marcuse's *One-Dimensional Man*, and other books and periodicals—all of a sociopolitical nature. Acorn's reading was a promotion for his book, *More Poems for People*. Sadly, the cover portrait of Acorn by Greg Curnoe was a grotesque embarrassment, as though it had been sketched on a wet napkin, in a tavern, by an unsteady hand. Anyway, the reading took place at a community center in the city's east end, in an industrial neighborhood of frame houses, dingy taverns, and soot-blackened factories. Although the venue was a far cry from the catered wine-and-cheese auditoriums in most universities where poetry readings are usually solemnized, it couldn't have been more in keeping with the strong, rhetorical spirit of Acorn's socialist poetry and his honest concern for working-class people. Moreover, it was the perfect setting to give his appellation "The People's Poet" free rein.

The audience on that evening was certainly a motley one. When I walked in a few minutes before Acorn was scheduled to read, I wasn't sure if I had stumbled upon a pep rally or was in the wrong place. Of the forty or so people present, there were women (some with children), girls in their teens, and neighborhood dudes who wandered in off the street, curious to see what a poet looked like. There were a few workmen in work clothes; some pensioners; some students, and others just standing around looking nonchalant. I had expected to see the university's English faculty there, but only professor-poet Eugene McNamara had decided to attend.

The room itself was a gymnasium-cum-lounge with a barbell-dumbbell set and weight-bench in one corner. Acorn slouched against the lectern, his book in one hand, a cigar in the other. A billiard table stood behind him. He wore a plaid shirt with the sleeves rolled up at the elbows, blue jeans, and scuffed work boots. If truth be told, he looked like a lumberjack just in from the bush. The audience easily related to him, probably because he wasn't condescending or pretentious—like the literary type who clasps his book to his chest as though it were a sacred text. After reading the first poem, Acorn muttered something, tossed the book over his shoulder and recited his poems. I marveled at his inimitable gesture. Memorized poetry is the surest way of signaling a love of language. It certainly grabbed the attention of the audience. They listened as he declaimed:

> Take a rain trip. Neither swallow it or smoke it,
> But stand out in the rain in shorts loin cloth or naked
> With every aperture of your body open
> And your thoughts a bubble from horizon to horizon.

This stanza of hexameter and heptameter near-rhyme line ends is a technical triumph. The proletariat had found an earthy kindred spirit in "The People's Poet," and quite a few people trooped out of the building with an inscribed discount copy of Milton Acorn's book.

Note: According to James Deahl—Milton Acorn's friend and indefatigable Boswell, *More Poems for People* sold thousands of copies. Deahl is also Acorn's "unofficial" literary executor.

2.

As time moves forward, and space and time become compressed, and societies become totally plugged into technology and seldom socialize in the flesh, I sometimes find myself wistfully conjuring up the past.

As a poet, I've appeared in several anthologies with Milton Acorn. Besides the first edition of *Whale Sound* (Douglas & McIntyre, 1977), the most attractive anthology (in format) was *New American and Canadian Poetry*, edited and with an Introduction by John Gill. It was published in hardcover and paperback by Beacon Press, in Boston, in 1971. This out-of-print anthology was the first of its kind to feature a selection from the works of Canadian and American contemporary poets. Photographs and biographical notes of the poets were included. This is what Milton Acorn had to say in his bio note at the age of 48.

"I was born in a small province, Prince Edward Island, somewhere about the same time as Jack Benny. I like to call myself an Indian, with some justification (the poems and biographical sketches about me invariably refer to me as 'red'—it means more than my ruddy color and even more than my politics). I am also Scots, Welsh, Portuguese, not in that order, and with some damnable English too … which I have spent my life denying. I simplify it by saying I'm a thousandth generation Canadian. There is such a thing and from it Canadians can take assurance that their nation really does exist.

"I worked as a carpenter for many years, but the alienated conditions in the trade (though I was a good carpenter) drove me to nervous breakdown. I in fact had published some poems while a carpenter; but the necessity (being a Canadian fully indoctrinated with the work ethic) of justifying my existence entailed me then becoming a good poet. I'm Old Left, merging on New—have sometimes been accused of being anarchist. The Allan Gardens Free Speech Fight, and *The Georgia Straight* are both in part my doing. Unlike most of the Canadian Left I can point to some successes; but what does that mean while millions starve? Nevertheless it has been that factor of success in my political work which has led to accusations of anarchism. In order to be a good Canadian Leftist you have to be a total failure.

"I was influenced in mid-career by Charles Olson's 'Projective Verse.' However I was equally influenced by my own study of poetic history, which revealed that the good poets wrote about the concerns which involved most people. Their highest concerns. Also I have studied imagery intensely, learning that the secret of imagery is looking at things with your own eyes. Also the line and the voice are much my concern. Also the void—not saying too much—leaving gaps and vistas down which the reader can look with his own magic eyes."

Notes: The Allan Gardens Free Speech Fight in Toronto refers to Milton Acorn reading his poetry to a large crowd in July 1962 to protest a bylaw that prohibited speeches in public parks and lead to serious debate over freedom of expression. Acorn shouted his famous poem, "I Shout Love," that ends with a battle cry: "Listen, you money-plated bastards. When I shout love, I mean your destruction." Acorn was ticketed and fined by the police.

When I lived in Toronto (the Good) in the spring of 1961, puritanical blue laws were still in effect. Restaurants, movie theatres, department stores, etc. were closed on Sundays. Public entertainment and recreation were verboten. In those days the city was white and uptight. A street in downtown Toronto is named Temperance.

The Georgia Straight was an "underground" newspaper that Acorn co-founded in Vancouver, B.C. in 1967.

"Projective Verse" was a project masterminded by teacher-poet Charles Olson and partly funded by Black Mountain College in the 1950s. Its objective was to free tight verse from its "closed" form, and project the poem like a projectile in an "open" field by using the "breath line," with short or long breath pauses, not counting caesuras, at the end of each end-stopped or run-on verse line. Because "projective" is also a psychological term, there was some confusion. A few faculty members and some students thought it was a new track-and-field event, or something related to yoga or deep breathing exercises. Vancouver poet George Bowering was so inspired by Olson's postmodern poetic theories, that he started a mimeographed magazine called *Tish* (an anagram of shit) devoted to examples of "projective verse." Enough said.

3.

My review of Milton Acorn's *The Island Means Minago* appeared in 1975. The Literary Press Group of Publishers reprinted it by permission of *Books in Canada*. Accompanying the review was a photograph of Acorn with disheveled hair, swollen left eye, gap-toothed smile, and holding a stogie in his right hand. This is what I partly said:

The Island Means Minago is Milton Acorn's eighth collection of poems. His first, *In Love and Anger*, he self-published in 1956. Although not as prolific as some of his contemporaries, his books have made a lasting impact on Canadian poetry. His latest one is about Prince Edward Island—its history and its folklore. (A "pussycat name" for a province, he said, because the island was a British colony in the 1700s.) "Minago" is the name given to the island by the indigenous Micmac people.

> Indians say a musical God
> took up his brush and painted it,
> named it in his own language
> "The Island."

Acorn has interspersed old and new poems with dialogue, chunks of prose, a periegesis of the province, archival photographs, and a scene from an unpublished play, *The Road to Charlottetown*. There are passages of such lyrical, rhythmical, and rhetorical power that one finds it difficult to associate the unkempt poet in the photo with the finished craft of the poetry inside. Perhaps there is a reason for this in a stanza from "I, Milton Acorn," a poem influenced by Bertolt Brecht, but with more metrical variations.

> The spattered color of the time has marked me
> So I'm a man of many appearances,
> Have come many times to poetry
> And come back to define what was meant.

I could continue quoting Acorn's poems for pages, but his poetry is (or should be) well-known enough without me having to give it my critical approbation. *If he's not the best poet in this country right now, I'll break my typewriter.*

After Milton Acorn won the Governor General's Award for *The Island Means Minago*, his publisher, NC Press, produced a large glossy black-and-white poster of Acorn's photo with my name and italicized blurb on it. Also on the poster, Acorn had scrawled with a ballpoint pen: *For Len. I hope you don't have to break your typewriter*, and his name.

Postscript: In 1972, my longtime friend Ed Bruski—a Toronto artist and high school science teacher—collected some of my poems and prose excerpts from source books about Pelee Island, which is the most southerly inhabited region in Canada. He said the material would make a nice booklet, and that he could do some drawings for it. I mulled over the idea. I wasn't altogether satisfied with the poems. They seemed unfinished. I needed to revise them.

A month passed. Bruski and I lived in two different cities and communication between us was desultory at best. I appreciated his proposal but I didn't share his eagerness to have a book. So, imagine my shocked surprise and mixed feelings when he showed up at my door one day with a cardboard box of books in his arms, smiling broadly.

"Who paid for the printing? Why didn't you let me know?" I asked.

The cover design looked attractive in green and black. The title: *Pelee Island Poems*, and our names (his for the fine drawings he'd done)—but hell's bells! The book didn't have an ISBN!

Fast-forward a year later to Grossman's Tavern in Toronto. Milton Acorn, Ed Bruski, and I are drinking draft beer, or rather they are. (I'm a rye whisky man.) We present Acorn with an inscribed copy of our book. He thanks us.

"I used four lines from your 'Island' poem* as an epigraph," I tell him.

He looks at it, immensely pleased. We drink a toast.

"Nice job; good drawings," he says, going through the book. "I like the tugboat poem."

"I'm revising some of them," I say.

"You're always revising," says Bruski.

"Thistle Printing, eh?" says Acorn. "Have you ever read *A Drunk Man Looks at the Thistle*?"

To make a long postscript short, it was *Pelee Island Poems* (a slight, weak book I disowned) that gave Acorn the idea for writing *The Island Means Minago*. I got it straight from the horse's mouth soon after the poster began appearing in bookstores.

One day I ran into Acorn at College and Spadina. We went to the Crest Grill for coffee, and he said to me: "You know, that little book of yours gave me a kick-start and got me thinking. I was born on an island, and I decided to go all out and put my heart and soul into Minago. And that's what I damn well did. Yeah, that's what I damn well did."

"You were in full sail, Milt," I said. "You put P.E.I. on the map."

* I first read "The Island" in *I've Tasted My Blood* (1969). Acorn revised this poem, adding an 8-line stanza to it. The new version appeared in *The Island Means Minago*.

4.

Jackpine Sonnets was a masterstroke of a title for a book in which Milton Acorn prescribed freedom for the sonnet. Acorn himself told me about his idea for this unusual collection. We were in his room one evening at the Waverly Hotel near Toronto's Chinatown, talking shop. I'd brought a bottle of Hungarian red wine, and he was drinking three glasses to my one. I was supposed to interview him for a magazine. The interview never happened. (Milton disliked formalities of any kind.) But I certainly learned about the irregular form, rhyme, and meter of the "jackpine sonnet," and even more about his politics.

First of all, Acorn's room was messy with books, magazines, and wastepaper. It reeked of cigar smoke, not to mention my cigarettes. But I didn't mind. A big Canadian flag draped one wall. There were three manual typewriters: Remington, Royal, and Underwood. When I commented on them, he said: "I use two for poetry and one for prose." Which made perfect sense to me. I mentioned that a songbird called the jackpine warbler nested in stands of jackpines in northern Ontario. Of course he knew this, but was impressed that I knew it too.

Acorn's lengthy introduction to *Jackpine Sonnets* is titled "Tirade by Way of Introduction." He states his case vehemently but partly tongue-in-cheek. "I do acknowledge that poetry is in a state of crisis and offer a partial prescription …" Then he veers off course. "Everyone knows I'm an ideological poet and my central ideology is Marxism-Leninism."

Politics aside, what should concern us are the joltingly innovative poems of this man. They add new dimensions to Canadian poetry, and give it a good sandblasting in the process. Also, he has taken the traditional sonnet and reworked it by dispensing with the fourteen-line straitjacket of its form and the different rhyme schemes of the Petrarchan, Spenserian, and Shakespearian sonnet. In other words, he has given it a freer form in the manner of Robert Lowell's unrhymed blank verse sonnets, and aptly named it after one of his favorite trees—the jackpine, "which can grow in any earth ... and having no set form, it makes all sorts of evocative shapes."

These free form sonnets cover a wide range of subject matter, varying in mood, and swirling with life's "eternal state of fission." The imagery is rich with metaphor and topical allusion. Sometimes dissonant lines cast a flickering light of their own. The seventeen-line, revised sonnet "Rose in Absence" lyrically transcends any rationale of human love, giving it an essence that is at once fundamental and intensely personal:

> The orgasm doesn't end. This moment
> Is like mated swallows spinning strands of time;
> Miniature cyclones in my breath
> Where exhalations from two nostrils blend.
>
> There was a man who told me dialectics
> Contradicted mathematical laws.
> I should tell him love's equally wicked.
> In a love-gift, what the hell's lost?

To digress a little, I think critics and reviewers have overlooked Acorn's corpus of love poetry. Perhaps they've been sidetracked by his public image of a working-class nationalist and socialist poet, as well as his political poems. In truth, Acorn has written some of the best love poems in 20th century North American poetry.

There are other sonnets that suddenly explode like a pyrotechnic display full of sound and color shot with irony. "Hope Begins Where False Hope Ends" is one of them. "Love in the Nineteen Fifties" is another. Sometimes Acorn adopts a combative stance, as in "The Craft of Poetry's the Art of War." There is no mincing of words in this anthem: "Put on your hardhat of proletarian scorn; / And when you throw roses—never mind how sweet; / For sweet life's sake don't omit the thorns." In "No Music from the Bar," the last line strikes a chord for neurotics: "Sleepless in Toronto—home of the homesick"; though nowadays it would be the "homeless." The sociological element in Acorn's poetry is always just below the surface, like a reef.

Included in the book are two whimsical, socio-political tall tales. Although both are amusingly anecdotal, they tend to detract from Acorn's inventiveness in grafting new stylistic forms onto the old regular sonnet.

Finally, the Jackpine is both metaphor and metonym for poet and sonnet—poet tree, if you will. "It has a basic form, yes, but grows to any shape that suits the light, suits the winds, suits itself"—the same way Acorn suited the zeitgeist of the 1960s and 70s. However, suffice it to say that his political didacticism didn't help his poetry. Ideological poet? For shame!

As I was getting ready to leave, I wanted to quote someone whose name I couldn't remember, but who said: "Ideologies were invented only to give lustre to the leftover barbarism which has survived down through the ages, to cover up the murderous tendencies common to all men." But I didn't.

5.

In the late 1970s Milton Acorn was a tormented man—"self-tormented," said some of his friends. Acorn's behavior sometimes skidded unpredictably in public—especially at poetry readings. This condition was attributed to his alcoholism and bouts of deep depression. His bohemian lifestyle also took its toll on him. (In many ways he reminded me of the American "Beat" poets of his generation.) He lived on the income from his writing, his disability pension, and the occasional Canada Council writing grant. For most of his adult life he was chronically impoverished.

I can recall reading poetry with Acorn, Ted Plantos, Bronwen Wallace, "Lord" Alfred Rushton, and others at the Church Street Community Center in Toronto back in 1979. It was a festive, disorganized, marathon affair, and the audience numbered about a hundred. Don Sedgwick wrote up the event in *Quill & Quire*, and singled out Acorn—not for his poetry but lack of propriety:

"Milton Acorn, the 'people's poet,' caused quite a stir early in the program when he launched into a tirade aimed at his fellow poets. 'I teach poetry at three schools,' he bellowed, 'and listening to these poets, I recommend a number of them attend!' He added: 'You don't hire a carpenter if he can't work.' After an argument with a member of the audience who taunted him for his outburst, Acorn was finally persuaded to recite his poetry. 'I'm going to read a naive poem but not nearly as naive as some I heard this evening.' He stumbled through several poems, then left the stage in disgust."

I was glad my turn to read followed his exit.

How do we appraise the mood swings of Acorn's behavior? He took poetry very seriously. It was his life work, his refuge from rage. He was the real thing: a true, hardworking, full-time poet. He didn't want to listen to poetry being anthropomorphized, euphemized, moralized, sentimentalized, trivialized ...

(I once heard him remark that Canadian poetry never went crazy. It was not meant as praise.)

6.

Time: 1980. Place: The Selby Hotel, Sherbourne Street, Toronto.

There is a very close connection between reason and emotion. Thus I've headed this anecdote like a dispatch from the front.

Patrick Lane and Montreal poet Artie Gold were in town. Come evening, they were going with Milton Acorn to the Selby Hotel for drinks. I agreed to meet up with them. I hadn't seen Lane since the year before, when I invited him to my apartment in High Park for dinner. He mentioned that he stood a good chance of winning the Governor General's Award for his *Poems, New and Selected*, and he borrowed twenty dollars from me. (Lane's book along with mine had been savaged by poet and critic Louis Dudek in a *Globe and Mail* review under the title THE POET AS RAPIST.) I last saw Artie Gold three years ago when I was in Montreal, and he proved that he was still the hot-dog eating champ of "the Main."

At the time, my friend Lenny DeFilippo was staying with me as a temporary arrangement till he found a place of his own. His wife had recently left him, taking their two kids with her, and leaving no forwarding address. He was restless and looking glum. I persuaded him to join me. "They're poets," I said, "and they like to drink."

Lenny and I had met through a mutual friend some years back. He was a year older than me, had a sturdy, athletic build, and was born and raised in the Bronx, New York. He moved to Canada on a student visa to study theology at Assumption College, in my hometown. He couldn't hack all the dreary Roman Catholic dogma, so he majored in psychology instead. "My karma ran over my dogma," he was fond of saying. Anyway, he married a Canadian girl and they later moved to Toronto, where he got a job as a social worker at a detention center for boys.

When we entered the crowded rathskeller-like bar at the Selby Hotel, I tried to locate the trio of poets. Then I saw Lane waving his arm. Lenny and I went to their table, sat down, and introductions were made. We quickly emptied a pitcher of beer. Lane signaled a waiter for another. They were revved up and enjoying themselves, with Acorn doing most of the talking and gesticulating. As odd man out, Lenny's presence seemed to cramp their style. They had been talking about the League of Canadian Poets—"plague" of Canadian poets, as Acorn referred to it. Lane asked Lenny if he was a writer. Lenny shook his head. "I'm a social worker," he said, and asked a waiter for a double bourbon. Nobody said anything. I tried to inject some levity, or something outrageous into the conversation. I mentioned that Lenny was originally from New York City.

Acorn pricked up his ears and said: "You made the right choice coming to Canada."

"I was trying to place your accent," Lane said. "I was there once, years ago. I arrived stoned, and left drunk."

"Yeah, the right choice," said Acorn. "You escaped from capitalist imperialism."

I reminded myself that Acorn was fiercely anti-American. (He had once written a wild essay on what the odds would be if Canada waged war against the U.S.).

"I'm not into politics," replied Lenny. "Most politicians are crooks."

"You got that right," said Artie Gold.

"To quote Thoreau: 'That government is best which governs least,'" I intervened.

"OR NOT AT ALL," Acorn roared.

"Here it is—1980, and Canadians are still subject to the quaint notion that only the government is qualified to sell booze," said Lenny, and raised his empty whiskey glass.

"We're more laid-back in Montreal," said Artie Gold.

Our talk seemed to drift and eddy around in the beery air like the smoke from our cigarettes and Acorn's cigar. Some funny remarks were made about Joe Clark's prime ministership. I sensed that Lenny was uncomfortable. He didn't have much in common with them. His knowledge of Canadian poetry was next to nil.

"Is it true that Hemingway stayed in this hotel?" asked Artie Gold.

"So they say," Acorn said. "Hemingway could've been a symbol of defiance to the evil genius of his own land, but he was a cosmic quitter; he had to be a Hemingway hero, like every one of his heroes ..."

"Milt, you're quoting yourself again," Lane said.

Acorn winked and raised his glass. "Little Morley Callaghan knocked him on his ass in Paris."

"Hemingway killed wild animals for sport," I said. "It would have been fair play if the elephants, lions, and rhinos had guns."

"The American psyche's still hung up on its manifest destiny," said Acorn. "Americans think they're the most important people in the world. American capitalism. It's like a starfish; it eats and shits through the same orifice. The land of greed and home of the knave."

"I wouldn't say that," Lenny cut in.

Acorn's eyes glinted. "Why not? It's a fact."

"Have you ever traveled in the States?"

"I wouldn't set foot in that country," Acorn said. "I've always been suspicious of Americans who immigrate into Canada."

"That's your problem, not mine," said Lenny. "How did you feel about American draft dodgers during the Vietnam war?"

"C'mon, you guys, take it easy, slow down, drink up," Lane said.

"We opened the door to them. I doubt if the U.S. would have done the same for us," said Acorn.

"You're dodging the question," said Lenny, as they eyeballed each other. "How did you feel about all those draft dodgers. Or don't you remember?"

Acorn bristled. "They did a noble thing by NOT fighting for a corrupt imperialist government that committed mass murder and used chemical weapons to destroy crops and poison Vietnamese civilians and water supplies ..."

"So, you empathized with the draft dodgers; but you're contradicting yourself when you tell me you hate Americans. What if your sister married one?"

Acorn suddenly flung his beer at Lenny's face, got up from his chair and lunged at him. Lenny countered, and they began shoving each other and swinging their fists. A chair overturned, hitting Artie Gold's knee. A half pitcher of beer and three glasses crashed to the floor. Lane and I tried to separate them. Artie Gold sat there, rubbing his knee, looking stunned. Two waiters hurried over to our table and ordered us to leave immediately. Nearby, several patrons were standing, observing the ruckus.

Lenny and I walked out ahead of them. I didn't know what to say, so I said nothing. "I shouldn't drink with drunks," Lenny muttered.

Outside, the cool night air felt refreshing. Lane and I tried to negotiate a truce between them. Acorn would have none of it. He was still fuming. We tried to calm him down, but he pushed us away. Then he attacked Lenny again. They threw a few body jabs at each other. Lane, Artie Gold, and myself managed to manhandle them and break up the fight before one or both of them got hurt. "I can see the headline: *Poet and social worker brawl over politics*," Lane joked, trying to ease a tense situation. Nobody laughed. Acorn and Lenny refused to shake hands. I bid the trio goodnight. We went our separate ways. Acorn, Lane, and Artie Gold headed toward the parking lot. Lenny and I toward the subway station.

In 1981, when I was living in Vancouver, doing odd jobs and reviewing books for the *Vancouver Sun*, I ran into Patrick Lane at a poetry festival. Together we recalled the scene at the Selby Hotel.

"I've often wondered, Pat, if I should have filled you in beforehand about my friend."

"Why?"

"Well, his wife and kids had just left him ..."

"That happens."

"Yeah, OK. Well, he grew up in an environment very different from yours and mine. You see, both his father and older brother are mafiosi in a New York crime family run by Joe Bonanno. My friend doesn't advertise this fact. He's bewildered by it, even ashamed. You might say he's the white sheep of the family."

Lane gave me a funny look. "Can I ask you something?"

I nodded.

"Do you choose your friends? Or do they choose you?"

"It all depends how you look at it," I said, and let it drop.

The Universe Ends at Sherbourne
& Queen (and Other Street Corners)

> *The conscience of a blackened street*
> *Impatient to assume the world.*
> —T.S. Eliot

Ted Plantos was the busiest poetry activist I ever knew. At first, I knew him by name only. I met him when I moved to Toronto in 1974, and saw his activism first-hand. Besides running Old Nun Publications, which he founded in 1972, he was also conducting poetry workshops and organizing biweekly poetry readings at the Parliament Street Library or "the House on Gerrard" as it was sometimes called in Toronto's Cabbagetown district. Ted invited me to read there a couple of times. I met other Toronto poets: Pier Giorgio Di Cicco, Robert Priest, Jane Jordan, and Alfred Rushton whom I later nicknamed "Lord."

Ted and I became good friends. We had much in common. We were born during World War II; we came from an urban working-class background; we left school at 17; we worked at a variety of blue-collar jobs; and each of us had published three or four slim books of poetry. Ted's books have imaginative titles that read like verses: *The Seasons Are My Sacraments, She Wore a Streetcar to the Wedding, All the Easy Oils of Energy* ...

Let's fast-forward to 1977—the year Ted Plantos published his first major collection of poems and prose: *The Universe Ends at Sherbourne & Queen*. An apocalyptic title, to be sure, but the intersection is in Cabbagetown, and the black-and-white photograph by Angeline Kyba on the front cover is disturbing, and in the style of Diane Arbus, which is more than a hint of what to expect when you read this powerful book. Except for Juan Butler's *Cabbagetown Diary* (1970) and Margaret Gibson's *The Butterfly Ward* (1976), both prose fiction about poverty and mental illness, *The Universe Ends at Sherbourne & Queen* was the first book in the history of English Canadian poetry to broach the subject of the underprivileged. Here's the title poem in full:

This is one of those ragged winters
when the old men cluster together
inside mission walls, listening
to their bodies groan with the wind
that flies like an axe through stone and snow

:one of those rheumatic winters
when all old warriors
who left their medals behind in pawnshops
gather at the torn edges of parks,
and pass the bottle from mouth to mouth

This is one of those winters
when the frost settles on the bones,
and each face betrays the war they could not fight

And the wolves at their feet have ceased howling,
their fangs rotting one by one
like the desolate row on row of beds
that stink from the loss of dreams

This is one of those Niagara winters
when some of the old men and some of their bottles,
stuffed between pillows and mattress,
won't make it past the morning

I daresay the poem gives you pause. It was pure coincidence that my review of Ted's book appeared in a slightly altered version in *The Toronto Star* on Christmas Eve—his birthday. Steel Rail Publishing in Toronto published it. The book was priced at $5.95. Compared with today's book prices, it was a steal. Here's the review:

Despite the home renovations and the increase of property values in the late 1970s that are gentrifying Cabbagetown, giving it a trendy and moneyed face-lift, the area essentially remains run-down though different from the Depression-era Cabbagetown that Hugh Garner described in his classic novel as "the largest Anglo-Saxon slum in North America." Cabbagetown's boundaries have changed over the years. In the map drawing (with numbered place names) that prefaces Ted's book, "Cabbagetown extends from Wellesley St. south to King St. and from Jarvis St. east to River St." Whereas its original boundaries were Gerrard St. to the north, Queen St. to the south, Parliament St. to the west, and the Don River to the east. Be that as it may, Plantos' book deals in spades with the indigent inhabitants and depressing aspects of that area. His poems and prose vignettes exude the reek of greasy spoons, taverns, pool rooms, and shabby roominghouses. We encounter the damage wreaked by poverty, petty crime, alcoholism, and welfare pogey; in short, the clamminess of dead-end lives fated to drift like debris in the gutters of human existence. A stanza from "Old Indian Woman in Allan

Gardens" poignantly evokes a mood of ironic dignity that transcends the squalor she lives in:

> Plastered on a park bench,
> toothless old Indian woman …
> before morning chokes you with frost,
> you will climb to the ground that chased you here,
> and walk back, inside yourself, to a pride
> that will peel you,
> in layers of white civilization,
> from the spirit trampled by progress

There are a number of strong poems, such as "A Bruised Performer," "These Moments Are Black Ink, "Losing the Wheel" and a long biographical discourse on "The Legend of Red Ryan"—a notorious Canadian gangster in the early 20th century. (I remember telling Ted that Red Ryan's life had all the ingredients that would make a great movie. Hollywood would have capitalized on his criminal career. He shrugged and said: "There's no film industry in Canada. Do you know any screenwriters? I don't.") These poems combine grim humor with pathos. Plantos' tone is neither vague nor sentimental; and his imagery, which can be unsettling at times, may take some readers out of the usual reader comfort zone. But his compassion for the down-and-outer always overrides the subject's loss of self-worth. Truths are presented realistically in the anomalies and miseries of life. The punctuation is minimal; the poems never end with a period, indicating that they all flow in succession. Whether writing about prostitutes or panhandlers, winos or the mentally ill, Plantos avoids sensationalism and *nostalgie de la boue*—or degradation for its own sake.

Of the prose pieces, "Stan's Complaint" is a masterpiece of working-class monologue. It is vivid and spontaneously profane, as if it had been tape-recorded in a factory. The excellent photographs by Angeline Kyba certainly complement the text. One photo in particular suggests the strangely fascinating hold that sleaze sometimes exerts on us.

That same year Plantos also published a poetry chapbook, *The Light Is on My Shoulder*; and two years later he co-edited an anthology that featured the work of fourteen Toronto poets. It was titled *Poems for Sale in the Street*, also published by Steel Rail.

Rereading Th*e Universe Ends at Sherbourne & Queen* compels me to digress on a more personal but relative note. I can remember when vagrancy and loitering were against the law in Toronto in 1961. Was it a by-law? a sly-law? Who knows? I found out the hard way. In March of that year I was evicted from my third-floor room in an old rooming house. I had five dollars to my name, no job, and no visible or invisible means of support. I took shelter from the wind and cold in an all-night laundromat on Yonge Street. The laundromat was empty, but it was warm. I was lying on a bench when two cops walked in. They checked my ID, questioned me, and then booked me on suspicion of vagrancy. They drove me to the Don Jail where I spent the night in the drunk tank, though I was cold sober.

In the morning I was directed to the Salvation Army Hostel on Sherbourne Street. Two scruffy-looking men smoking cigarettes were loitering in front of the hostel. "Hiya, kid," one of them said. I nodded and went inside. A man in a Salvation Army uniform signed me in, told me the rules, and issued me a bed and two meal tickets—one for lunch and one for supper. Muddy coffee, unbuttered toast, skinny bologna sandwiches, watery vegetable soup, gooey macaroni and cheese, Jell-O.

In the dormitory-like room that night, some down-and-outer in the cot next to mine had his right foot in a dirty plaster cast. He kept scratching himself. "Bedbugs," he said. He kept me awake all night with his farts and groans.

As soon as it was daylight, I fled the hostel.

I hitchhiked back to my hometown.

In this day and age, the universe not only ends at Sherbourne and Queen streets but at thousands of city street corners in North America. Homelessness has reached a crisis. There is no affordable housing. Rental prices are extortionate. The homeless (formerly "vagrants") are ubiquitous. "Tent cities" and city street corners now house the homeless. The streets are rife with crime and fear. Racism is on the rise. I know many people who are in debt. I'm one of them. Debt is a profitable thing for creditors whose long-term interest rates must be the envy of loan sharks. Blame corporate globalization; economic globalization; capitalism. GREED. The history of economic progress consists of charging a fee for what was once free. Everything on which communities depend has been seized, privatized, and commodified. (The way things look today with global warming and such, there could be a military struggle among the superpowers for control over the world's natural resources.) The middle class was a buffer zone between the rich and the poor. Burdened with insurmountable debts, the middle class is crumbling, and there is an ever-increasing polarization of wealth. If we were all created equal, programs for achieving equality wouldn't exist. The poor have always wanted to get to the top and the rich have always refused to step down. This natural phenomenon has been going on for three millennia. What are YOU going to do about it?

Ted and I saw each other regularly over the years, and we kept in touch by snail mail when I lived in other cities. He remained active as always in literary projects, namely, as co-editor of *Cross-Canada Writers' Quarterly* and *Poetry Canada Review*. For recreation we sometimes went to a baseball diamond and played catch, and took turns hitting fly balls to each other. He continued to publish poetry, short stories, articles, and book reviews. Three of his last books were *Mosquito Nirvana* (1993), *Daybreak's Last Waking: Poems Selected and New* (1997), and *The Shanghai Noodle Killing* (2000). The last-mentioned was his first collection of short stories. As a storyteller, his social consciousness permitted him to comfort the afflicted and afflict the comfortable.

Ted identified with the street. He had street savvy. In fact, the word "street" appeared many times in his poetry and prose. I think it was his lodestone. Growing up in Cabbagetown probably had something to do with it. He once took me on a walking tour of Cabbagetown, pointing out its old Victorian-style houses, the Royal Oak Tavern, the New Service Tea Room, St. Paul's Church, and other landmarks. The tour, with a rest stop for drinks at the Winchester Hotel, inspired me to write a short poem called "Streets," which I dedicated to him. I think the poem appeared in "Lord" Alfred Rushton's *Gut* magazine.

> There are streets that follow us
> wherever we go; streets
> that run our lives day after day;
> streets that corner us at night
> when we are lonely or alone;
> and there are streets that get lost too.

Ted Plantos died on February 20, 2001. He was 57. I was a pall bearer at his funeral.

The Third Poetry

Consider these traditional Japanese lyric forms:

An old silent pond ...
A frog jumps into the pond,
Then silence again.
　　—Bashō

Disturbed, the cat
Lifts its belly
On to its back.
　　—Karai Hachiemon

So sweet the plum trees smell!
Would that the brush that paints the flower
Could paint the scent as well.
　　—Rankō

All three are vividly concise in their perception of natural imagery. They exemplify objective realism, responsible vision, and intuitive insight, especially with regard to natural imagery. Influenced by Chinese and Japanese poetry, Ezra Pound coined the term "Imagism" in 1912, and then promoted it. Amy Lowell followed suit, and a movement began. Other so-called Imagist poets became fascinated with haiku and tanka poetry. Their experimentation with image and metaphor laid the groundwork for modern poetry and its attendant free verse. In fact, Imagism has been described as the grammar school of modern poetry.

In the 1950s and 60s, the Beat poets—especially Jack Kerouac and Gregory Corso—contributed to the haiku's popularity. Here is one of Kerouac's: "What is a rainbow, / Lord?—a hoop / for the lowly." And Corso's: "A bluebird / alights upon a yellow chair / Spring is here." Black poet Etheridge Knight nails it down: "Making jazz swing / in Seventeen syllables AIN'T / No square poet's job." Canadian haiku-meister George Swede published a short but informative book, *The Modern English Haiku* (1981), which is sadly out-of-print.

And yet, concerning nature, how far did modern poetry really go? Or for that matter, modern prose fiction? Anthony Huxley, botanist and author of *Plant and Planet* (1974) said that poets spend more time looking at themselves than observing the natural world around them. Virginia Woolf wrote: "Novelists have very little love of nature. They use nature almost entirely as an obstacle to overcome or as a background to complete, not aesthetically for contemplation or for any part it might play in the affairs of their characters."

To deal with nature in poetry is to deal with nearly the whole task of poetry; for poetry is, to paraphrase John Dryden, *the image of nature*. Yet there are poets writing today who sometimes make the egregious error of attributing human feelings to birds, trees, and other natural objects. It seems poetry has always lived on this anthropomorphism. The so-called universal analogy stems from it. Even John Ruskin who coined the phrase "pathetic fallacy" sometimes made a pathetic slip. So ingrained is pathetic fallacy in the psyche, that Linnaeus misnamed the black-capped chickadee—*Parus penthestes*, of which the binomial means grief or sorrow, because of the chickadee's black cap. In our time, we name hurricanes after people.

Here is an Arabic ghazal titled "Dates" by an anonymous poet, translated by E. Powys Matthers. It is a beautiful synthesis of nature and art.

> We grow to the sound of the wind
> Playing his flutes in our hair,
>
> Palm tree daughters,
> Brown flesh Bedouin,
> Fed with light
> By our gold father;
>
> We are loved of the free-tented,
> The sons of space, the hall-forgetters,
> The wide-handed, the bright sworded
> Masters of horses.
>
> Who has rested in the shade of our palms
> Shall hear us murmur ever above his sleep.

Most nature poetry, especially poetry about animals, is simplistic, opportunistic, and exploitive. Poets use animals in poems as we use them in so many other ways: in labs, in agriculture, in fashion, as exotic pets. We use them as metaphors, as vehicles for our own concerns. We don't realize that nature is its own metaphor. To my mind, Canadian poets Milton Acorn, Pat Lowther, Patrick Lane, and Andrew Suknaski write about nature with perceptive realism. Lane also had a kind of self-reckoning in the cultivation of his garden, and green-thumbed his way to G.M. Hopkins' "freshness deep down things."

The reasons for the flabby use of pathetic fallacy are manifold: the mind-body split codified by Christianity, conceptual semantics, urbanization, animal cartoons, the onslaught of technology, ignorance of the natural world, romantic doubts about nature, because, as a term, nature is usually thought of by modern writers as an ambiguous word. There is another reason too—a pernicious one—which I shall pinpoint later.

It was Henry David Thoreau who said: "How much is written about Nature as somebody has portrayed her; how little about Nature as she is." Which brings me to my theme—"the third poetry" of Walter Anderson (d. 1965), a reclusive Mississippi artist, naturalist, and writer who spent most of his life painting and writing about the flora and fauna on the Mississippi Gulf Coast and its barrier islands. He accomplished that third poetry of which he wrote: "The first poetry is written against the wind by sailors and farmers who sing with the wind in their teeth. The second poetry is written by scholars and students and wine drinkers who have learned to know a good thing. The third poetry is sometimes never written, but when it is, it's by those who have brought nature and art together into one thing."

The dominant note in Anderson's "third poetry" is the judgment of egocentricity, indeed of anthropocentrism. Anderson believed that what wastes the beauty of nature is the deflected eye of human subjectivity. In this Anthropocene epoch of high technology, few will understand Anderson's homage to natural objects as few have any experience of objectivity, and most deny the very possibility because of their indifference to the natural world or their superficial knowledge of it.

Several books of Walter Anderson's artwork and writings were published after his death. His *Horn Island Logs* is a worthy match for Thoreau's *Walden*, but with one difference. He went beyond Thoreau in his relationship with nature, accepting nature's terms more completely. Anderson didn't moralize or sentimentalize what he saw and experienced. He was nearly fatally snakebitten in a mangrove swamp. He once lashed himself to a pine tree in order to experience the full effects of a hurricane. (The only poet I can imagine doing that is Hart Crane.) Anderson's logs help us to see things with a new perspective, and, more importantly, to realize that we humans are just one species among nature's infinite objects. We have constructed too many walls between ourselves and animals. We and the other species of the earth have a relationship in need of serious therapy. As it is, we are not only alienated from the natural world, we are becoming alienated from one another. Even worse, we are conditioning ourselves to become an abstraction. American author and animal rights/environmental activist Randy Malamud says that "art can and should have a direct ecocentric impact."

I read somewhere that American and Canadian poets tend to center their writings on themselves. Could it be that this tendency is not so strong in Europe, because there it is counterbalanced by historical experiences. Poet Robinson Jeffers said: "I'd sooner, except the penalties, kill a man than a hawk." However, the conditional pause in his assertion nullifies the intent.

Some years ago, Canadian poet Salvatore Ala published an unrhymed sonnet titled "Pathetic Fallacy," in which he announces: "Due to toxic levels of pathetic fallacy/Bookstores have been closed by the Board of Health." Oh, would that it were true. Depending on how words are used or misused, the most noxious landfill can be language itself. Of course a child can be excused for saying a bird is happy or a flower looks sad, but an adult poet—*Never!* As a figure of speech, it's pathetic. An Eisteddfod ought to revoke his or her poetic license. But let's not go overboard.

Conversely, Samuel Johnson, ever the ironist, advised against numbering the streaks of the tulip. Granted; but if you're hunting for Indian arrowheads, you must look for a stone that wanted to fly.

Since grammar is the basis and foundation of all human knowledge, poetry imposes a certain order on thinking. Form is responsible for that, as well as cadence and diction. Synecdoche makes possible the intense compression of images, as art and nature are enjambed. Verlaine took rhetoric and wrung its neck. As regards pathetic fallacy, I can't recall Homer, Dante, and Shakespeare stooping to such untruths. Yet Burns, Blake, Wordsworth, Shelley, and Keats delighted in it. Tennyson diminished its use. Dylan Thomas used it with surrealistic and Welsh bardic effectiveness. Rimbaud synesthetically colored the vowels; declared: "Everything we are taught is false"; gave up poetry at 19, and became a gunrunner and slave trader in Abyssinia. So, where does that leave "poetic truth"?

Poets have their own versions of "truth"; but it would take an undaunted and discerning reader to explore the relation of these truths to the truth of actual reality. Which is why science and poetry since the time of Plato have been at loggerheads over the problem of knowledge; and since grammar is the basis and foundation of all human knowledge, the error of poetry is one that involves nature. It is analogous to the necessity of hypothesis in science. Perhaps the only basis for a mutual understanding can be found in the very substance of poetry: metaphor, which is a bridge from the minor truth of the seen to the major truth of the unseen. The haiku and the urban pastoral might be useful examples. Thoreau noted that "the bluebird carries the sky on its back." A vivid metaphor! "Seek those images that constitute the wild," sang Yeats.

Like the mind-body split that defines Western culture, the dualism between science and poetry, humankind and nature, happened because of religion. And it originated in *Genesis* (chapter 1, verse 26) of the Old Testament: *"And God said, Let us make man in our image, after our likeness: and let them have dominion over the fish of the sea, and over the fowl of the air, and over the cattle, and over all the earth, and over every creeping thing that creepeth upon the earth."* What arrogance! What anthropocentrism! Patriarchal in the extreme. Small wonder that sea, earth, and sky are polluted, and that so many wildlife species are extinct or in danger of becoming extinct. (Newfoundlanders once slaughtered seals. Japanese and Russian fishermen slaughter whales and dolphins. In the 19th century, the megalomaniac King Leopold II of Belgium funded the wholesale slaughter of elephants for their ivory in central Africa. Buffalo Bill gained his nickname for killing 4,280 buffalo in eight months). Consider the appalling conditions to which we consign our fellow creatures: zoos, public aquariums, animal circuses, a three-tiered tractor hauling a hundred squealing pigs to the abattoir.

Perhaps the root of the problem lies in our Latinized binomial nomenclature: *Homo sapiens*. (More arrogance.) What if the epithet *sapiens*, which means *wise*, consisted of only the first three letters: *Homo sap*. (Don't snicker.) Would that difference have changed our nature? We have a tendency to form our beliefs first and then go looking for evidence to support them, rather than the other way around. How else can you explain the fact, which I read in *The Economist*, that more people believe in angels than in Darwin's theory of evolution? Evil, after all, is a human thing, like the Devil—a Judeo-Christian concept. We've been shackled by the bible and by those who use it as a tool of power. "How can I trust them," wrote Gregory Corso, "who pollute the sky/with heavens/the below with hells."

Hart Crane has a fragile lyric, "A Name for All," that epitomizes the fragmentation of the natural, and human, world:

> Moonmoth and grasshopper that flee our page
> And still wing on, untarnished of the name
> We pinion to your bodies to assuage
> Our envy of your freedom—we must maim
>
> Because we are usurpers, and chagrined—
> And take the wing and scar it in the hand.
> Names we have, even, to clap on the wind;
> But we must die, as you, to understand.
>
> I dreamed that all men dropped their names, and sang
> As only they can praise, who build their days
> With fin and hoof, with wing and sweetened fang
> Struck free and holy in one Name always.

Ecology has become a modern eclogue between nature and us. Ecologically, our feet are already stuck in the muck of our own making, and the water's rising. Our natural resources are rapidly diminishing; and NAFTA is a smoke screen for sweatshops. Although hope lives in doubt, there is some hope, and awareness. In 2009, Wilfred Laurier University Press published *Open Wide a Wilderness*, edited by Nancy Holmes—the first anthology to focus on Canadian "nature poetry" in English. Also, there are numerous books of *ecocriticism* that focus on ecology, natural history, and humanity's relationship with the natural world; and "nature" writers such as Rachel Carson, Edwin Way Teale, Farley Mowat, and Sir David Attenborough come to mind.

Ah, the natural world of mammals, birds, reptiles and amphibians, fish, invertebrates, insects, trees and shrubs, wildflowers, nonflowering plants, and mushrooms. Let us try to see them in the wild, not from our point of view, but from theirs.

Acknowledgements

Books in Canada, The Pacific Rim Review of Books, The Prairie Journal, The Toronto Star, and *The Windsor Star*.

An unrevised version of a hundred or so lines of Götterdämmerung appeared without my knowledge or permission in the *Canadian Poetry Review* in September 2018.

About the Author

Len Gasparini is the author of twenty-one books of poetry, short stories, and essays. His work has been translated into French and Italian, and anthologized in Canada and the U.S. He has lived in Toronto, Vancouver, New Orleans, and Washington State, and now resides in his hometown of Windsor, Ontario with his wife, writer Lisa Pike, and two calico cats.

Recent Books by Len Gasparini

The Social Life of String (2018)
Collected Poems (2015)
Mirror Image (2014)
The Snows of Yesteryear (2011)
When Does a Kiss Become a Bite? (2009)